15 MINUTE MBA ADMISSIONS APPLICATION:

Nailing the Personal Statement

Jovi Brown, PhD

Jovi Brown

> "Life is like riding a bicycle. To keep your balance, you must keep moving."
>
> —ALBERT EINSTEIN

The *15 Minute MBA Admissions Application: Nailing the Personal Statement* is a resource tool to help aspiring MBA students write effective personal statements on their admissions applications. It started out as a 15 minute short read; but, after the author added more advice and over 30 tips, the book is a 45 minute short read packed with relevant insight and examples.

Copyright ©2019

Jovi Brown, PhD is CEO of Top Brainiac Inc. and enthusiastic about business, technology, and helping others to add value in the workplace. She has taught business management, motivation and leadership, and applied artificial intelligence technology.

Dr. Brown can be reached via e-mail through the website www.topbrainiac.com or directly at jovi.brown@topbrainiac.com or via phone 229-352-9531.

DEDICATION

This book is dedicated to all who have inspired, pushed, and/or supported me to keep moving as well as all who aspire to keep moving in the business world.

CHAPTER 1

So, you're applying to an MBA program at Nice University, and it's time to write the personal statement. I've researched the MBA application's personal statement and successfully coached applicants to write personal statements that hit not only the points that the admissions committee looked for but also helped the applicants stand out from others.

The object of your personal statement is to sell yourself. You're on the block. You're up for sale. You want Nice University to be the highest bidder and buy you.

Think of your personal statement as responses to interview questions. When you physically have an interview, you choose relevant, powerful examples to sell yourself to the company. For example, when you interviewed for your current position, you provided short, relevant examples to demonstrate your strengths and, to an extent, weaknesses. Of all of the stories that you could have told, you chose the ones that you felt would make the hiring manager say, "Let's hire her" or "He's the one for the job"; and, when you told the story, you made it short, sweet, and to the point.

It's the same way with the personal statement. You choose examples that you feel will make the admissions committee say, "Let's accept her" or "He will add value to our program", and you briefly tell the stories in a convincing manner.

Overall, you want to organize your personal statement in three "sections"—past, future, and present. You want to tell your past. Then, explain your goals. Follow that with showing them why you need their MBA to achieve those goals. I know that past, present, future is the general norm for writing; but MBA programs like the past, future, present format. As a note, you won't label sections in your personal statement.

CHAPTER 2: PAST

At most, the past section should be 40% of the essay and provide a good depiction of your career history in terms of career experience and extracurricular activities that depict success, development, and relation to future goals. Though this section is called the past, it includes present job history.

Remember, the admissions team will already have your résumé, so you don't want to re-hash résumé material. Speaking of the résumé, tailor your résumé to the admissions committee's needs. Sometimes, you can get a feel from admissions information and/or representatives on the career experience and extracurricular activity—such as relevant society memberships, volunteer work, internships, and the like—that the team looks for in ideal candidates.

Provide short, powerful examples of your career success. Remember the relevant stories. You want to vividly show the admissions team that you've had a successful career. Tell professional milestones that you've overcome, accomplishments, industry insight, and the like. If you advanced to your current position faster than most people, then make sure to state it somewhere. Remember, you're selling yourself.

Have your career related stories show progression and development. Though you pick stories that show forth your best, make sure that the stories show that you're more of a leader and thinker now than when you started your career. Again, keep the "Let's accept her" thought in mind.

Make sure that your past and present career stories relate to your future goals. This helps to show another level of progression. Namely, your past and present are preparing you for the future. This could be practical preparation or theoretical (transferrable skills).

CHAPTER 3: FUTURE

In the future section, articulate your short and long-term goals, and demonstrate how they relate. This includes your short term plans for directly after graduation, why you'll succeed, why you're needed, and what you'll do after you accomplish your short term goals. Spend time in this section—roughly 50%.

Short Term Goals

Articulate your short-term goals in terms of what you intend to do right after graduation, why you'll succeed, and why you're needed. You don't have to tell it in the order presented.

After Graduation Intentions

Tell what you intend to do right after graduation. State the specific job title that you see yourself holding—and if known at a specified company. This should be a real job title at that given company.

Mention a few duties you see yourself doing. These should be real duties for that position at that company.

Remember, you're trying to show that you've done your homework. You've looked into your near future, and you've chosen a specific position at a given company. You've seen yourself in the near future, and you look better. You know specifically how you'll be better in doing what.

Why You Will Succeed

Tell why you will succeed in that position/industry. Note the position you've held in the past and/or knowledge that you have about the industry that will give you insight. You're not bragging, but you want the admission's team to know that you plan to be successful; and you can already see it.

Why You Are Needed

Tell why you are needed in that field. State specific steps you'll take to overcome the industry's problem(s). Indicate that your MBA from Nice University will give you the specific skills —strategic planning, decision analysis, strategic leadership, and the like— that you need to overcome the industry's problem(s). Derive these skills from your program's course titles and descriptions. Choose a few relevant skills.

Example

As an experienced Beekeeper, I understand that many bee farms often have a shortage of honey in the Spring due to inefficient marketing strategies, marginal employees, and low financial resources. With my MBA from Nice University, I will have the requisite strategic marketing and operations management skills needed to develop a bee farm to its fullest potential. As such, after earning my MBA from Nice University, I see myself in my first position as the Operations Manager at Mrs. Brady's Bee Farm, strategically marketing organizational strengths, implementing efficient operational policies, utilizing intellectual and financial capital for growth, and expanding sales into national and international markets.

Long Term Goals

State your long-term goals by building upon your short-term goals. Tell what you would like to do after you achieve your short-term goals. You don't have to know exactly. This is how you ultimately see yourself. This is the distant future.

Example

In the long term, I would build on my bee farming success by acquiring multiple bee farms that need strengthened operations. To accomplish this, at Mrs. Brady's Bee Farms, I would climb the corporate ladder to become a Portfolio Manager. In this capacity, I see myself helping acquired companies by strengthening their management teams, improving intellectual and financial capital, and making effective marketing decisions. Ultimately, I would like to own a company that specializes in acquiring bee farms that need strengthened operations, and I would use my portfolio management experience gained from Mrs. Brady's Bee Farms to make my company successful.

Summary

The key here is to be honest and build logically. Tell them what you really want to do in the future, and show them how your short-term goals tie to your long-term ones.

CHAPTER 4: PRESENT

In the Present section, portray value—contribution. Show that you've researched the MBA program, looked through course descriptions, viewed statistics, toured the campus, and/or talked to students; and tell the admissions committee how the information furthers your interest in the program. Also, tell the team specifically how you will add value.

Your Connection

Give the admissions committee insight on your connection to Nice University's MBA program. This is where you share your feelings about what's drawing you to attend and how those attributes can prepare you for life after graduate school—the real world.

Why You Want an MBA

Tell Nice University why you want an MBA from them. The goal here is to show them that you've done your homework on them. You know that they have specific courses, hands-on training modules, programs and/or other specific resources that can help you achieve your goals. You'll look at the course and program descriptions and write how the specifics will help you.

Example. I am interested in improving bee farm operations, and Nice University's executive management program resonates with me in that its New Ventures Program, Strategic Marketing course, and Operations Management for Critical

Change class would prepare me to thrive in the industry. Through the New Ventures Program, I would spend three weeks in a hands-on training environment facing a real organization's operations challenges and using the help of peers to problem solve and develop solutions. This would prepare me for potential challenges that I could face in improving bee farms' operations.

In Professor Sally Satterfield's Strategic Marketing class, I would learn how to scan the environment for weaknesses, opportunities, and threats so that I can help position bee farms for competitive advantage. Also, in Professor Adam Martin's Operations Management for Critical Change course, I would learn to integrate quantitative analysis with strategic principles to guide bee farms through organizational change, allowing the farms to transition from underperforming (shortage of honey in the Spring) to high performing (surplus sales in national and international markets). Notwithstanding, Nice University's academic programs would challenge and prepare me for success in bee farming.

Why You Are a Good Fit

Also, tell them how you're a good fit for their program. You want to show the personal connection to the school. Here you can discuss information that resonated with you from conversations/interactions with alumni, students, staff, faculty, and/or admissions. Also, if you've visited the campus, then you can mention your impressions of the campus.

Example. When I visited Nice University, I was really impressed by the academics as well as social life. I enjoyed Professor Pitney's Strategic Organizational Leadership 501 course and found her explanation of the relationship between leader mental clarity and organizational effectiveness interesting. Also, I had a great time with students Isabel Jones and Gary Street who took me all over campus, made sure that they answered my questions, and ended our day at Café Loco where they introduced me to tens of students. With the sound academic atmosphere coupled with the amazing social networking, I had a wonderful time and felt at home. I look forward to attending Nice University and becoming part of such a great community.

How You Will Contribute

Make sure to tell them how you will contribute to their program. Let them know how you'll contribute to the school's nonacademic programs; i.e., clubs, school events, student organizations, and the like. Also, you can discuss how your intangible qualities would contribute to the school's atmosphere: 1) your confidence and enthusiasm which stems from family support throughout life could help you bond with classmates and take leadership roles, 2) your ambition and determination which allowed you to overcome challenges as an undergraduate and still earn your bachelor's degree could give you the drive to complete their program within two years, and 3) your past work experiences could help you enrich class discussion with relevant examples.

Example. Outside of the classroom, given interest in bee farming, I would like to become a part of Club A which specializes in helping small businesses. Perhaps, I could use my connections in the bee farm industry to help strengthen the club's agriculture committee or Annual Street Fest where local businesses are invited to purchase booths and sell items.

Also, I would add value to your program's social atmosphere. Throughout life, no matter my endeavors, from little league baseball to State University to my current position at XYZ, my family has been my number one support. They have instilled confidence and enthusiasm for life in me. Because of these qualities, I easily make friends. As such, as a learner, I would actively engage in course room discussion and talk kindly with my peers.

Why Their Program Now

Tell them why you want an MBA now. What will their MBA do for you? Though you don't want to state another university's name, but when answering this question, you may want to think of how their program could help you more than a different program. How is their program positioned in the competitive landscape, and what value would that add to you?

Example

Attending Nice University will position me to succeed in the bee farming industry. My experiences inside and outside of the classroom will prepare me to help improve bee farm marketing strategies and operations. While in school, I will gain insight to help bee farmers, and this will solidify my case study discussion in the classroom. After graduating, an MBA from Nice University could position me for competitive advantage in the marketplace.

Summary

You get the point here. Some of the information overlaps, so pick and choose what to use. You want your contribution section to show that you know specifics about the program. You'll add value, and the program will benefit you (in some cases, benefit you so that you can add even more value).

If you run into a jam on word length and need to cut words to fit within the stated word maximum, then the contributions section is the section to trim. Don't completely delete it. Rather give enough to show that you'll contribute and move onto a quick summary.

CHAPTER 5: NOTES AND COMMENTS

Overall, make your personal statement personal. You want your voice to come through so that the admissions team can feel your experiences, commitment to your field, and desire to earn your degree at their university.

Keep your work experience stories relevant. Tell what you really want to do in the future and how an MBA from Nice University can help make that happen. Show them why it's them and not their competitor that can help you realize your purpose. Within that, make sure to tell them what you'll add to make them stronger.

In the appendix, see more relevant tips. Until next time, take care of yourselves and your education. Hope you the best!

APPENDIX

Though it sounds redundant, you want to make your personal statement—well—your personal statement. Make it authentic and a good writing piece. Proofread, proofread, and proofread! Here are 30 more random tips:

1) Check for grammar, style, and punctuation mistakes. Submit your essay only after correcting mistakes.

2) Have someone read and critique your work.

3) Be you. After reading your work, the committee should have a sense of who you are.

4) Stay within the given word limit. Don't write one word over the limit.

5) Comply with all instructions. This is not the time to win innovation points and create a new way of doing things. If they give instructions, then simply follow them.

6) Let your writing voice come through so that the team can hear you and get a sense of how you might respond in classroom discussion.

7) Demonstrate that you value experiences that have gotten you to where you are—even if you took the nontraditional route or the road less traveled.

8) Keep it relevant. Only include job and industry information that add to examples about you and your experiences.

9) Try to write a different personal statement for every business school to which you apply. Even if they ask for the same information, try to change something in order to keep the writing fresh.

10) Tell what happened. Don't lie.

11) Show them how you've used your setbacks to set you up for better. You triumphed over trials. Yay for you!

12) Don't submit your résumé as an essay. (Yawn) Boring!

13) Stay on point. Answer the questions asked. They don't need to know what happened in the 8th grade or how many cupcakes you eat when stressed.

14) Take breaks. Step away from writing and come back to keep the writing fresh. Even if you're a weekend warrior, breaks can help.

15) Remember that spellcheck is your friend. Spellcheck!

16) Demonstrate leadership skills.

17) Progress the writing. If you've already said it, then don't keep saying it. Let go of redundance.

18) Highlight professional achievements—especially current ones.

19) Don't try to sound like a business school AI robot. Sound personable.

20) Brainstorm. Write all that you can write before you trim for final production.

21) Make your first sentence one to remember. Start with a quote, story, statistics, or something that will grab attention.

22) Give yourself plenty of time to write. Don't put this off until the last minute and try to cram. You want time to think clearly.

23) Know your why, and convey it. Even when you're not directly telling the admissions committee why you. To an extent, your whole statement should tell them why you.

24) Choose relevant, powerful examples to sell yourself to the admissions committee. In case you skipped reading the book, I emphasized powerful examples.

25) Search for jobs that require an MBA, and look at the job descriptions. Promote your knowledge, skills, and abilities that resonate that you are MBA material.

26) Balance professional word choice with personal voice.

27) Breathe. You can do it. You've accomplished so much, and this too shall pass.

28) Believe. Keep a positive mindset while writing. It will

help you to stay positive in your statement.

29)   Paint vivid pictures. You want the admissions committee to envision your examples as well as you in their program.

30)   Read, read, and re-read the book *15 Minute MBA Admissions Application: Nailing the Personal Statement*. The book is filled with tips to help you succeed.

Jovi Brown

AUTHOR'S ADMISSIONS GUIDE RECOMMENDATIONS

15 Minute MBA Admissions Application: Nailing the Personal Statement

15 Minute MBA Admission Application: Résumé Quick Reference Guide

The information in this book is to be used as a guide for individuals preparing to enter MBA and other programs. Suggestions are based on the author's professional and educational experience as well as research. The author does not guarantee that individuals who adhere to the information contained in this book will get accepted to any MBA or other programs.

AUTHOR'S BIO

Jovi Brown, PhD's Bio: Passionate AI technology, business management, and innovative leadership, Jovi is CEO and AI Engineer at Top Brainiac Inc. In the past, she served as an MBA admissions coach, business speaker, advanced analytics enthusiast, researcher, and business instructor as well as management consultant with technology skills in data science, big data, and predictive analytics. She earned her BS from Vanderbilt University, MS from Florida State University, and PhD from Capella University. jovi.brown@topbrainiac.com

www.ingramcontent.com/pod-product-compliance
Lightning Source LLC
Chambersburg PA
CBHW031941170526
45157CB00008B/3271